AF480901

THE ESSENCE OF ENLIGHTENMENT

NEHA TALELE

The one who is the material cause of creation, whose unique manifestation as Samsara has its existence, who hold sway over all beings, He, who is the most important factor in the generation of this universe, who is free and is therefore one's own master, whose nature, greatness & actions cannot be known by anybody, who hides one's own nature with the help of His power of Maya, I pray to you,

Oh! Shri Hari Narayan

Contents

Karma Yoga: The Path Of Dynamic Action

  1. Karma Yoga — 3

  2. Dynamic Action In Crisis Moments — 5

  3. The Spiritual Science Of Karma Yoga — 7

  4. Understanding Leela — 9

  5. Efficient Problem Solver — 11

  6. Dharma — 13

  7. Wisdom In Action — 15

  8. Unattached Actions — 17

  9. Be Bold To Evolve — 19

  10. The Philosophy — 20

Raja Yoga: The Royal Path To Bliss

  11. Raja Yoga — 25

  12. Krishna's Approach — 27

  13. The Yogic Attitude Of Harmony — 29

  14. Control — 33

  15. The Inner Being — 35

  16. Bliss — 37

  17. Courage — 39

  18. Slaying The Demons — 41

  19. Conquer Your Fear — 43

Bhakti Yoga: The Path Of Devotion

  20. Bhakti Yoga — 49

  21. The Power Of Devotion — 50

Contents

22. Surrender   52

23. Faith   54

24. Strength   56

25. The Power Of The Subtle   58

Gyaan Yoga: The Path Of Knowledge

26. Gyaan Yoga   63

27. Trapped In Thoughts   66

28. Decisiveness   69

29. The Cosmic Mind   71

30. No Limits, No Boundaries   74

31. Being Neutral   76

Ultimate Warrior Consciousness   79

Karma Yoga: The Path of Dynamic Action

CHAPTER ONE

Karma Yoga

If your consciousness is in a good state, you have taken the greatest leap towards dealing effectively and efficiently with tough times. Krishna says: *"The person who is free and non-attached, whose mind is established in spiritual knowledge, does all actions and all work as sacrifice."* In other words, Krishna looks at action in life as a spiritual means to something higher. The first thing is, within yourself be free! Within yourself be unattached. Within yourself be aware of the mind-body-spirit dimension of life, and do all work as if it is an offering to the greater power of the universe that Krishna represents. Then you'll find that all your actions dissolve into being effortless. And if you can tackle all challenges and untoward situations in life with this attitude of inner spiritual freedom, there is nothing to fear. You become empowered, you become luminous in the way you tackle things. Not only do you become supremely calm within yourself, tranquil and still, but you also find a bliss underlying your very being.

The supreme warrior is one who can fight even against the toughest enemy without a feeling of vengeance, and with the feeling that he just has to go and do his or her best. If you fight the battle well, that is enough. You don't have to physically win it. The true winning of life's battle happens in the domain of the mystical, the spiritual. Which is why Krishna, in the Bhagavad Gita, reminds Arjun that the whole idea is to fight the battle and not worry about what will happen thereafter. What happens thereafter is in the hands of the Lord; it's in the hands of the greater power.

Arjun has become emotionally and mentally weak before the Kurukshetra war. Feeling pity for those he is going to kill or maim in battle, he has put down Gandiva, his bow. Krishna exhorts him to pick up the bow and fight. Krishna even shows Arjun his absolute and ultimate form—his cosmic form called the Vishwaroopa. But before that, he explains to Arjun how the idea of acting freely and luminously itself takes one to a transcendence of all crises.

Krishna teaches Arjun the secrets of true yoga. He says: *"You become a yogi by renouncing desire for the fruits of action."* Within this line, you find the whole crux of the concept of Karma Yoga! Act without thinking about the results. In that way, you become unfettered, liberated, fearless, full of wisdom, spontaneous, effortless, and most importantly, your most natural self! So acting, you have the best chance to come out of tough times in a blissful manner. And ultimately, all of life is—in Krishna's perspective—looked at as a great battlefield where life and death don't matter as much as the way you fight. It is your inner being, your consciousness which matters.

CHAPTER TWO

Dynamic Action in Crisis Moments

Arjun is facing a deep crisis! At an individual level, he feels that he would be responsible for so much bloodshed should he fight as the great warrior he is. At the societal level, he feels that he would be setting a bad example for people to follow the path of violence. Krishna tells him that there is nothing to worry about, because eventually, Arjun is fighting a battle for justice. He is, in fact, fighting for societal good. Hence, he is simply to give his very best. He is to wield his bow just as Krishna wields his flute. Let the melody of life play through his actions naturally, without anxiety. The idea and lesson for us when faced with our own crisis moments is this: ***Don't get caught up in your own little anxieties so much that you are unable to fulfil the task that you are born for.***

Each of us is individually empowered with great talent. It is up to us to tap into it, to find it. Yet, most of us get stuck because we are too attached to results. We keep thinking about whether our work will be successful or not. Krishna's is the way of complete adaptability, of non-attachment, of being like water! When the situation demands it, water can adapt. It is as the great martial artist Bruce Lee said, echoing the Taoists' point of view, that water can fill any vessel that you put it in. It has this ability of adaptability. It is not stuck to its particular form. It is free-flowing. And Taoist philosophy is, at a very subterranean level, very influenced by Krishna's teachings.

Depending on the situation, adapt and act. Don't get stuck by what your mental conditioning is, nor by what you were thinking yesterday. Leave all that behind. Flow like water into whatever you need to do: into the crisis at hand, into the challenge at hand, so that you can solve it. Then you're able to act not only with efficiency, but with joy, strength, and power. Also, you are able to act without self-consciousness, without feeling the sense of the "I". In modern psychological parlance, there is the concept of "flow": the state of being from which you function freely, effortlessly. That is the ideal that Krishna is pointing Arjun towards. When faced with a challenge, flow with all your might. Don't hold anything back.

The Spiritual Science of Karma Yoga

Krishna tells Arjun: "O mighty-armed one, this spiritual science of Karma Yoga is difficult to attain without performance of free and selfless actions . . . But he whose actions are free from desire for results, he whose actions have been burnt by the fire of spiritual knowing, such a person is indeed like a sage." So the warrior (implying the person facing challenges in life) is also to act like the wise sage. That is the key to Karma Yoga. That is Krishna's counsel to Arjun.

This message of Krishna's is transformative. Arjun's mental blocks and defences melt in the face of it. Arjun feels like he can be his most natural and complete self only as a non-result-oriented warrior. On the other hand, if he doesn't face up to the challenge—if he doesn't rise to the occasion and fight the fight as he's meant to do—all his energies would be wasted. The lesson for us is this: to create such a flow of warrior-like and sage-like energy within that you act as a channel for the Infinite. That is the whole secret of Karma Yoga.

Krishna is teaching Arjun how to channel his entire energy into one of mind-body-spirit harmony. When that harmony is reached, then one feels that one has no limits. Else, one's mind keeps reminding one of what may happen and what may not happen. The main thing is to function as if all the different aspects of oneself—one's thoughts, one's emotions/feelings, one's material and spiritual aspirations—all play together like in an orchestra: different instruments, but coming in together to create a singular piece of music. Harmonious. Especially during tough times, it is very important to work like that.

Understanding Leela

When it comes to the concept of Krishna, there are a few aspects that are very important to understand. He is the eighth avatar of Vishnu, but in many ways, is the most important. He embodies the very essence of the concept of divine play or Leela, which is at the heart of Indian spirituality. Leela means that everything is created out of the pure bliss and playfulness of the Infinite (that Krishna is taken to be in his ultimate form). And knowing life to be a Leela is really the spiritual attitude we must take towards all difficult circumstances, challenges, untoward situations, tough times, and crisis situations in life.

Never feel hopeless in the face of tough times. Remember it's just another chapter—another act—that is going on in this divine play called Leela, orchestrated by the divine personality of Krishna. If you look at life like that, then you look at all your actions in your life as an actor would: detached from the role, knowing that your ultimate reality is higher than the material circumstances facing you.

Through this understanding, you are able to act materially freely also because you are not self-conscious anymore, you're not fearful anymore. You know you have to act your part as you must, in sync with what William Shakespeare said: "All the world's a stage, And all the men and women merely players." That is the very attitude we must take when faced with tough times. It is not only the correct, sacred attitude to take, but also has a deep psychological effect on us, because it takes us from the state of over-anxiety to a state of carefreeness.

And from the spiritual perspective, the carefree/blissful/surrendered attitude is very important. One simply moves on, does what one has to do: moving forward, not looking back, through non-hesitating action. Then one enters into the dimension of true problem-solving.

CHAPTER FIVE

Efficient Problem Solver

During tough times, we are required to solve tough problems. Yet, it is often our own complex web of thoughts which prevents us from acting dynamically, from acting with all the energy that we are capable of. Don't keep questioning yourself: true courage can never arise when you become doubtful about everything. For courage to happen, you have to have an inner state of relaxed acceptance, non-attachment, vitality in inner being, and ultimately, a feeling of *Ananda* or divine bliss. If you have these qualities within you, you automatically are able to meet with circumstances as they must be met with.

That is what Arjun eventually does. He's filled with bliss and confidence by the end of Krishna's message in the Bhagavad Gita. Krishna tells him very emphatically that only the person who acts selflessly, purely, with senses under control, is the one who's truly acting freely. Such a person is working efficiently even without seeming to work. Such a person has become a problem-solver most effortlessly.

"Such a person," says Krishna, "feels and thinks: I am not doing anything (i.e. only the greater is working through me) . . . And it is the performance of this kind of action which is superior to renouncing action." Here, we can see Krishna putting the very core and very pith of his message in perspective. And his message is very different from what Buddha and other ascetics of India have said. They have asserted the renunciation of action, the giving up of that which seems morally incorrect.

But Krishna teaches in a very different manner. He says: "The person who can act in an effortless way, playing his or her part in a state of inner flow, is actually doing something superior to the ascetic who seems to have renounced action." The idea is, if you can act without any motive of attachment to results, you become empowered, because you are acting in an objective manner. And eventually, when it comes to decision-making during tough times, when it comes to good objective thinking and clarity of perception, such a person is the one who can lead not only his own self but lead all of society also towards dynamism, towards a state of betterment because such a person is not acting out of limitations of emotion and thought.

The core lesson is this: Clear your thoughts and emotions. Act freely.

CHAPTER SIX

Dharma

Krishna says: *"It is better to be in one's own Dharma or self-nature than the Dharma of another. It is better to die in one's own Dharma. Being and working through someone else's nature or Dharma is the most frightful thing."*

The lesson is this: always be yourself while doing any action, don't try to imitate another. Your self-nature is your own; it is unique. It is your very duty in life to work according to your self-nature: this is a key understanding about Karma Yoga.

And again, Krishna says: "Work becomes pure when it is done as service to me. And he who performs actions, dedicating them to me, becomes like the lotus leaf that, while being in the water, is still untouched by the water." In other words, the purest action in life, the boldest action in life is that which is done with this ancient Indian analogy of the lotus in mind. The lotus exists amidst murky waters: yet it glows, it shines with its own colours, its own hues. Be like that! That is *Dharmik* action.

We are surrounded by the murky waters of life's unpredictable situations. What are difficult circumstances? What are crisis situations in life? They are like wading through a pool of murky water. Yet within ourselves, if the lotus flower is blooming—in other words, if within our being the consciousness is one of wisdom—one is able to go through these circumstances. Then you're able to act as you must act. You are able to blossom to your true potential. That is wisdom in action.

Wisdom in Action

Krishna says: "By action alone, King Janak and other great people realized great perfection. Be a good example to others, Arjun, in the performance of your action . . . The wise perform action in a state of non-attachment . . . They desire the welfare of all beings . . . Make others become devoted to work through performing your own actions properly." Here, Krishna is defining the very ideal of how a wise leader should work. Setting a good example.

Not only do you set a higher standard for yourself when you work selflessly, as the great King Janak did, you also become a spontaneously charismatic and important leader for others through your example. This is key to Karma Yoga.

You see, Arjun has fallen from wisdom into a state of utter doubt, a state of utter despair on the battlefield. He is not able to work at all. He's not able to walk the path in his natural nature, his Swadharma. His psyche has become paralysed. His courage has disappeared. The splendour of his warrior-like bravery has evaporated in the face of the crisis that faces him on the battlefield. A very small part of his energy is functioning. Krishna is enabling Arjun to bring the entirety of his energy into the essential task that is needed to be done on the battlefield. And Krishna is reminding him: "Be established in yoga, Arjun. Perform your actions by giving up attachments. Be unconcerned about success or failure. Don't do your duty prompted by desire. Do your duty prompted by wisdom. Take refuge in wisdom alone. That is yoga. That is skill in Karma. That is Karma Yoga. By abstaining from action, you will not reach perfection. Be devoted to your work . . . Be an instrument of my nature, because of which you have to act. You have no choice but to act as a warrior on the field!"

Krishna is taking Arjun away from the morass of negativity. Krishna is withdrawing Arjun from the idea of the destruction of his own body and the destruction of his enemies' bodies, into a state where Arjun can do what he has to do with a completely open heart and mind! The most problematic thing during crisis situations is that we close our hearts and minds—the proverbial heart within which resides our energy of courage, and the mind within which resides the ultimate consciousness and wisdom to do the right thing through thoughts, words, and inspirational action.

CHAPTER EIGHT

Unattached Actions

Krishna keeps reminding us of that kind of action which is truly liberating. He tells Arjun: "Perform action that is unattached. Through that, you attain the highest . . . Whatever a great person does, others follow . . . Set a good example . . . Think, Arjun, if I stop action, the whole world will cease . . . I have nothing to do in this entire universe. Still I engage in action . . . But remember, Arjun, take delight in the soul, be satisfied in the soul. So knowing, you realize ultimately, there is no action to perform. Yet, you may act."

Krishna is telling Arjun the ultimate principles about how to act properly. And he gives his own example as the procreator of the entire universe, as the "super-soul" behind all things.

He says that whilst he as Godhead has no real need to act, he still does! Else, the whole world will cease. And he also implies another very important thing: take delight in the soul. Delight or Ananda in the spirit itself is the ultimate search of human beings and indeed of all beings. If you realize that, you can act freely. There is ultimately no need to act, but action is a means towards spiritual liberation. It gives you the opportunity to realize all your mind-body-spirit energies, and therefore, to achieve that which you need to achieve in your life.

Ultimately, no achievement matters as much as the spiritual achievement of the meditative state, the blissful state that Krishna represents. And of uniting with that state. The negative attitude of renouncing action that Arjun has within him is really what precipitates the crisis even more.

CHAPTER NINE

Be Bold to Evolve

Be bold enough, dynamic, energetic and vital enough to meet each crisis with such strength of spirit that is truly courageous. Have a boldness that is flowing, that is able to take you towards higher evolution.

Moving towards higher mind-body-spirit evolution is the ultimate message of Krishna. And he's doing it not just at the individual level of Arjun, but rather doing it for the collective consciousness through the instrument of Arjun. He tells Arjun that that which Arjun does, others will follow. The lesson is this: if you want to be a leader of people, always remember that you have to set a good precedent by acting through a higher sense of wisdom, a higher sense of compassion and empathy. And empathy does not mean feeling pity for others. In fact, what he is telling Arjun is to go, which obviously implies killing the enemy. Yet, on a higher plane, such action is preferred to the other option: to abandon the war and to let others take the blame for the battle. If you are a responsible person, you'll have to take the responsibility upon your own shoulders!

CHAPTER TEN

The Philosophy

Krishna's approach of Karma Yoga is always more complete. Because he is able to address the situation not with a stereotypical answer, but instead with the need of the moment. Depending on the need of the moment, you have to determine your action. He's not saying that you have to fight with people who are peaceful: no! He's telling Arjun to fight with those who are already on the field of violence, who are already perpetrating great injustices on the people. Hence, Krishna makes complete moral sense also, because he believes in creating a balance through one's actions.

Where there is injustice, it has to be balanced by justice. Where there is physical catastrophe, it has to be addressed by physical means, rehabilitation, and so on. Where there is spiritual crisis, it has to be addressed through a psycho-spiritual approach. Where there is psychological distress, it has to be approached by psychological counselling.

In these ways, Krishna's approach to tough times and difficult situations in life is comprehensive. There exists no one singular answer. There exist all kinds of answers. The idea is to function from the very core of your being, from the pulsation of your spiritual energy. And when the answers come from the pulsation of your spiritual energy, all that you do to address the difficult circumstances/ challenges/untoward situations/tough times, takes you towards the non-disturbed, calm, and wise resolution of those problems.

• 21 •

Raja Yoga: The Royal Path to Bliss

CHAPTER ELEVEN

Raja Yoga

Krishna reminds us in the Bhagavad Gita that life is beset by problems. That life is in fact the greatest battlefield, within which each of us has to fight our own battles. Yet it is how we choose to fight the battle—in what state of consciousness we confront our challenges—is what ultimately matters! And the art of facing up to all our challenges and crisis moments through intuitively realized wisdom, and calmness in consciousness, is key. It is the path of Raja Yoga, the royal road to courage, success, and bliss.

The lessons of Raja Yoga are amongst the greatest learnings to imbibe from Krishna. Raja Yoga is an integrated yogic science of mind-body-spirit wisdom. Its ultimate objective is to remind us of one key thing: create supreme peace within yourself. That empowers you for all things in life, and helps you find union with your infinite self.

Through the understanding of Raja Yoga, there are three lessons to be learned especially with reference to life's challenges:

(i) Enhance your intuitive life force through energizing the vital life-energy called prana

(ii) Enter the intuitively meditative state, culminating in samadhi or enlightenment

(iii) Reach a transcendent state of energy and bliss, unlocking your inner super-consciousness and emerging an infinitely more empowered being.

The key things we are to remember about Raja Yoga are creation of inner peace and tranquillity, which spontaneously leads to courage and wisdom in the face of all life's fluctuating or changing situations, ultimately resulting in our highest happiness or ananda. Find the quality of unchanging, timeless peace deep within yourself: that is the secret of Raja Yoga.

CHAPTER TWELVE

Krishna's Approach

Krishna's approach is whole and integrated. He says, "It is only one amongst thousands of people who strive for perfection. And one amongst these only eventually knows me in my real form."

The objective is to point out the perfection, glory, and beauty of that mighty force of being which is represented by the Godhead; but is possible to us also because we exist as reflections of the divine. Krishna's approach is unique because it deals with life in all aspects—including life's challenges—and specifically emphasizes our duty to act according to our self-nature. Krishna says: "That person attains great perfection who remains devoted to his own Dharma."

Krishna is talking about how we are to remain true to that which is our self-nature, our swadharma. Again, Krishna says: "Whatsoever beauty or might exists, know that it has come from me. It is a small spark of my great splendour." Krishna is really telling us about how all things contain the very essence of his qualities. Within the sanctum of our being exists this greatness, this fount of wisdom, this royal quality which is all courage, all trust, all light. We are nothing less than the divine, though only reflections of it. It is like the moon on the water: while not the moon itself, the lake is able to reflect the light of the moon. So too do we reflect the light of divineness, of great power, of universal splendour. Knowing this is to find courage, and to be royal or king-like in our courageous approach to life's difficulties.

Even though we ourselves are not the ultimate being, yet we hold within our hands the ability to manifest that ultimate being's higher qualities: that "light", so to speak. Knowing this, all the falsehood from ourselves drops, all our cultivated sense of personality, ego, and so on becomes unimportant. What really remains important is that we know the source we come from. And that source is Krishna who represents Godhead. In that sense, we have no boundaries: we surpass all definitions of mind, body, and soul. We are really none other than the greatest truth. It is, as the Upanishads say, **"Aham Brahmasmi"**: the ultimate truth resides deep within us.

But what is the means to tap into this divinity, this greatly courageous or gutsy quality which has no limits? Krishna advises: "Learn to love the state of solitude. And in that awareness, think of me, ideate on me." Krishna is telling you about how you are to go into the cave of your innermost mind, your innermost heart. There, you will find your ultimate reserves of courage. There, you will find your ultimate reserves of divine quality. Tap into that. Then you'll find a great space of power within you. And when you find that space of power within you, you become indifferent to the small problems of the world. You are able to tackle them in a state of detachment. Else, crisis and tough times have a way of affecting us too much: we often become attached to them, and we are unable to come out of anxiety about them.

CHAPTER THIRTEEN

The Yogic Attitude of Harmony

The very core-essence of Krishna is the message of higher yoga. And the yogic attitude is basically coming to a great harmony with all of life. It means coming into a state of internal unity with all of life. In the Bhagavad Gita, the great text within which Krishna teaches the warrior prince Arjun the highest methodologies to overcome mind, body, or spirit crisis moments, Krishna says: "The yogi is greater than those people who practise austerities. The yogi is greater than those people who practice and absorb knowledge. The yogi is greater even than the person of action. Therefore, be thou a yogi, Arjun."

Krishna is guiding Arjun onto the harmonious path of Raja Yoga, the royal path. It is the idea that you move into an inner space which is imbued with spiritual strength, spiritual power, and, most importantly, spiritual harmony. You are to become unshakable—without limits—within your inner being. So doing, you can utilize all energy from within find expression and release for the resolution of any problem you face. Especially when you face difficult situations, especially when you face tough times in life, does the art of Raja Yoga truly come to use. Krishna, by the path of Raja Yoga, is emphasizing that intuitive and meditative state which takes us to our highest perfection. Nothing is perfect in life. But if there is one thing which is actually non-negotiable in Krishna's view: it is the idea of being meditative, no matter whom you worship, no matter whom you believe, no matter what you have faith in!

Real prayer, real fortitude, and real success in life is, in Krishna's vision, the meditative attitude. And the meditative or inwardly harmonious attitude towards life is the very essence of Raja Yoga. It allows us to break free of the bondage of conditioned thought. It allows us to leave all sense of inner aggression, inner anxiety, and to become simply a true instrument of the higher power. Through Raja Yoga, one acts as a king must act: the ideal king acts with a great deal of calmness, yet a great deal of control and authority. The great king acts in a manner which has grace within it, but at the same time has a firmness within it, a resolve within it. And most importantly, a good king has to act without fear. These are the very hallmarks of Raja Yoga which Krishna is teaching Arjun.

Krishna tells Arjun: "There is no destruction for the person who does good. Such a person does not come to grief . . . A true yogi making diligent efforts is purified and has his mind absorbed in Godhead . . . There is no doubt, Arjun, that the mind is restless, the mind is indeed hard to control. But by detachment and by continual practice, the mind can be controlled. Yoga is only hard for a person who cannot control himself. But it is easily attained by that person who has controlled himself and who makes an effort by the right means." Here, Krishna is summarizing the very essence of Raja Yoga. He's talking about the person who realizes the meditative attitude to be in a transcendence to material attachments. Don't be too attached, be detached:

that is the essence of real meditation.

What is the meditative state? It is one where you are not thinking too much of your attachments. You therefore are not imagining anxieties, gains, or losses. You are attached neither to the body, nor to the material factors, nor to attaining any spiritual or religious goal as such. You are free, unbounded, limitless—without any sense of being restrained. And in that state only can you be relaxed, in that state only can you be free, in that state only do you attain an inner restfulness of being. And it is only when you attain an inner restfulness of being that you attain your highest energy. Without inner restfulness of being, there cannot be an expression of your highest energy.

When faced with tough times in life, you need most of all, your highest energies to function harmoniously within you. You need to be luminous within yourself. You need to have a very broad spectrum of intelligence alive within you. And what the non-yogic or disharmonious state does is make us afraid. It narrows us. The yogic state, the state of Raja Yoga, is one where you are absolutely controlled yet absolutely free. In other words, you are, as Krishna says, "Like a lamp in a windless place which does not flicker. That is the yogi . . . This yoga should be followed with a non-disturbed, non-anxious heart . . . This yoga can be followed by being completely tranquil, by being quiet within, by being free from anxiety and strain, and identifying with the highest reality or Brahman. Then, real bliss and real happiness come to you."

Again, Krishna is emphasizing that meditative state which takes us to a feeling that all our anxieties have disappeared. And that is the very crux of meditation. You are to first of all drop all your human anxieties. You are to attain that state of your natural intelligence, free of conditioned thoughts, free of conditioned imaginations, free of conditioned patterns of behaviour. Then only does the doorway of the greater success of life open. Else, you keep repeating what you did yesterday. The mind keeps wandering. And the wandering mind is the enemy of man. As Krishna says: "When the mind wanders and is restless during meditation, take a grip on it. Be patient. And thereby, it becomes controlled."

CHAPTER FOURTEEN

Control

Krishna says, "The control of the mind is the highest yoga. The control of the mind is like controlling that boisterous, unruly horse which has to be tamed and made to obey the rider . . . Burn away all impurities in life by meditation. It is the only way! . . . Fix the mind. The yogi has the mind controlled . . . Yoga is not for the person who eats too much, nor for the person who eats too little . . . It is not for the person who sleeps too much, nor for the person who sleeps too little . . . Only that person who is temperate in food, in activity, at work, while sleeping and waking, attains yoga. And that yoga takes away all our sorrows."

Krishna is assuring us that the state of Raja Yoga makes us free of sorrow, liberates us. The mind is like an unruly horse: bring it under control. There is no need for the mind to keep wandering. You'd realize that in your own life, it's when the mind wanders into unnecessary anxieties is when you feel like you are not in control. You feel feverish in heart and mind. You feel uncertain. Certainty can only happen in the spiritual-dominated being. The logic-dominated being can sometimes make you imagine things which don't even exist in the first place. You keep wondering that something bad may happen in the future. And that state means the opposite of Raja Yoga. Raja Yoga means that you are willing to accept even the unfavourable down the line. And unfavourable things do happen in life. Don't be afraid, rather laugh at it. If you can do so, you become a higher warrior as Arjun became after hearing the divine Bhagavad Gita from the lips of Lord Krishna: he became far more steady in spirit. And the steadiness of spirit, with the steadiness of mind, are really the essence of Raja Yoga.

CHAPTER FIFTEEN

The Inner Being

Whatever our battle in life, we are all warriors. We are each fighting our own battle, within our inner beings as well as within the material world. Even if we are not renunciates, even if we don't have a very strict spiritual life, we still can apply what Krishna is talking about as the path of Raja Yoga and feel blissful, feel energetic, and stop feeling that things are a burden in life. Don't fear anything in life: that's the first thing for both warriors and renunciates. Drop the burden of fear completely. Then you move towards Raja Yoga with great speed. What it does is, it brings you towards a centredness of your own being. And centredness of your own being is the whole key. Why do you worry about material circumstances? Things will come and things will go. Yes, there will always be niggling worries at the level of body, at the level of your work, at the level of your relationships. That does not mean that you disturb your inner being.

The inner being within you should always be in a pristine state. And that pristine state is what Raja Yoga is all about. It gives you insight. It gives you the ability to see past the nervousness of the mind. It gives you the ability to become cognizant of all challenges, yet transcend the anxiety of those challenges through the meditative part of yourself. And in fact, the meditative part of yourself is the truest part of yourself. If you keep thinking about life as task-oriented, action-oriented, you actually don't reach to the innermost core of your nature. Action is always exterior. That which is interior-most is your intuitive meditative ability. It is the space of your consciousness. It is what determines your basic human ability or basic human quality. It is the root of yourself. You must water your own roots. That is what Raja Yoga is in the end!

If you water your own roots, you become intense, you become pure and effortless in the ability to meet with uncomfortable situations in life. Hence, it is said that the true yogi is one who is so rooted in reality that even the mightiest storm cannot shake him. And Raja Yoga is a method of catalysis. It is not about particular methods and particular techniques. Ultimately, what is needed is this idea to sink deep within you: that you are blessed with great inner potential, that your inner being is exceedingly valuable. Understanding its strengths releases its power. And that is only possible when you are able to go deep into it. Absorb the bliss of yourself.

Bliss

Self-bliss contains all the treasures that you need. Within you is all the highest ability, within you is all the capability for insight into reality, within you is all the essence of what various religious paths have taught in the past. You are a living embodiment of the highest potential. Never forget that. Never underestimate yourself. Raja Yoga brings you to a natural culmination of your self-potential. And then, you realize that you have just been simply too self-conscious all your life, too anxious, too nervous. If you drop all that, you come to your naturally focused and intense, blissful state of being. And that is the spiritual state of being. Within that spiritual state of being exists an innate power which allows you to take on anything in life without fear, without any sense of trepidation, without any sense of trembling.

Raja Yoga means a heart-to-heart relationship with the yogi hidden deep within you. Each of us has the ability to generate waves of fulfilment, contentment, bliss, success, spontaneous effort, and great power. Raja Yoga is telling you to realize this multi-dimensionality of yourself. You are not who you think you are. You are far greater! And this has nothing to do with ego. This has nothing to do with feeling superior, or inferior, for that matter. It is the idea that the true diamond exists within you, the true treasure trove exists within you. In the Raja Yoga point of view, each of us is a treasure trove of great energies. All we need to do is tap into those energies. That makes us tap into the eternal, the timeless, the all-powerful, the omniscient, the omnipresent, and so on. It is a contact with our deepest inner voice and our deepest inner power. And when you have that, there is absolutely no limits to what you can achieve, there are absolutely no limits to the whole expression of your self-potential.

Your very nature, your swadharma blossoms when you walk the path of Raja Yoga. And walking the path of Raja Yoga means you simply look at life as being one within which the intuitive or meditative state is more important than any other state: emotional, intellectual, and so on. Be content being you! Yet, the "you" that you think is your actual self is only a reflection of your deepest being. Within your deepest being, you have the power to remove all obstructions, you have the power to remove all hindrances that have kept you back. And when you realize this power through being meditatively intuitive, you can actualize this state of being within all practical aspects of your life. In the real world too, you then have the guts to face up and walk on, no matter how tough the fight looks. You don't exist in a negative state. You exist in a blissful, happy state, ready for challenges.

CHAPTER SEVENTEEN

Courage

What is real courage in life? Courage always stems from an inner state. Some people may not seem physically very intimidating, but they have a great deal of courage within themselves. In fact, great conquerors such as Napoleon and Alexander are said to have been relatively short people. Yet they never allowed their physical limitations to come in the way of realization of their self-potential. Now, Raja Yoga is not about being an Alexander or a Napoleon at all. It is about being an Arjun. But at the core of it really is to find inner contentment, inner non-tension, inner harmony, and spontaneous expression of all that you are capable of.

What has truth and purpose is identifying with the wellspring of meditative ability within us. When that becomes dominant in your being, the ability of tough times to affect you becomes weak. You are able to surmount difficulties. When you climb the "inner mountain", then you can summit any outer peak! That is the whole key of Raja Yoga. Krishna teaches: "You must have poise. You must have confidence. Maintain your equanimity, even if placed in difficult circumstances, in extreme circumstances . . . Never give back hatred where there is hatred, neither give back injury when you are injured. Desiring your greater good, strive to free yourself." Here, Krishna is teaching us that we must have poise within ourselves. We must have great faith. And at the same time, we must have equanimity of being, stability of being, stillness of being. That opens us up to a state where we do not react in a negative way. We react in a positive way. And that takes us towards higher good.

Krishna describes infinite truth and reality in a very interesting way. He says: "Truth has infinite aspects. And infinite truth has infinite expressions. The Rishis speak in many tongues, they speak in many ways. But at the end of it, they express the same truth." Krishna is telling us that though all religions are different in form, yet at their very crux is this courageous state of Raja Yoga. There are infinite ways to give expression to spiritual knowledge. Yet, at the root of it, at the foundation of it, lie the principles of Raja Yoga which he enumerates in great detail. And really, at the very heart of Raja Yoga is a transformation of consciousness. It's the evolution of ourselves from our base, animal instincts to our godly instincts. We are comprised of opposites! There is both the demon and the god within us. It is up to us which we want to manifest.

CHAPTER EIGHTEEN

Slaying the Demons

The path of Raja Yoga is one where you manifest your divinity more and more. And when you do that, you are able to slay all the demonic forces in life. In Indian mythology, all sorts of afflictions, all sorts of untoward circumstances are metaphorically known as "demons". To slay these "demons" is our highest spiritual duty. And throughout Krishna's life, there are metaphorical tales about how he vanquished various demons—Kaalia the serpent and so on. These are all ways of saying how we must maintain equanimity in our fight. Life is indeed a battlefield, as exemplified by the Mahabharat, the great epic of India. Yet to win this fight, you must be in this royal state of inner being where you are able to make the fount of wisdom flow forth into all your actions. When that happens, you attain the state of the yogi. And that state is one which is beyond the ego. That state is one where you attain an objective truth, where you attain an objective realization of your soul.

Krishna says: "When the individual realizes me, the super-soul of all, the problems within heart and mind are loosened, the doubts cease, and the individual is freed from karma." In other words, when we realize that godliness which is at the heart of the universal soul, then all our doubts disappear. We suddenly become free from the cause and effect of karma. The real way to blessedness in life is to move past this desiring and hankering after the lesser things and going towards the realization and super-consciousness of the highest being, as exemplified and personified by the personality of Krishna. Krishna says: "To have no desire is the highest good. Blessed is the person who has no desire." Forget all your myriad desires.

CHAPTER NINETEEN

Conquer your Fear

Krishna says: "The purpose of life is to reach immortality by conquering both life and death." This kind of "conquering" which he is talking about is really the conquering of our inner fears, our inner trepidations. It's very interesting that while the Bhagavad Gita is set upon the battlefield, Krishna is talking about not conquering the physical enemy so much. No! He's talking more about conquering the "enemy" in the guise of human weaknesses, human ego, the illusory pursuits that we indulge in. If we conquer those, we know the path of Raja Yoga. Then suddenly, heaven becomes available to us, joy seems real to us. Else, we are lost in so-called happinesses of the world, enjoyments of the world.

Raja Yoga tells us that the only real enjoyment is this internalized state of meditative bliss. If you go there, you attain victory or Jaya. The name of the Mahabharat in Sanskrit was originally Jaya or victory. And that victory of life is always through this path of walking, speaking, acting, ideating like the yogi does. The yogi does not calculate. The yogi does not do things out of a spirit of wanting to dominate the other. No! The yogi acts out of a spirit of wanting to unleash the highest that is within him or her. When that is done, contentment becomes more fully accessible in life. Without that, there is only misery; there is no happiness as such!

And the ultimate pursuit of human life is always happiness. In fact, it is bliss. In Indian thought, it is as has been mentioned before, pure Ananda. Ananda is the state to reach. Without Ananda, there is no fulfilment in life. Ananda means that intrinsic, inbuilt capacity within us which is of the nature of consciousness, truth, and ultimately, of bliss. Bliss comprises all. Within bliss lies the highest consciousness and within bliss lies the highest truth also. Knowing this, you are able to encounter all situations in the spirit of Ananda. Then, even tough times can be taken as a lesson, as a learning, and you are unshakeable because you are established in the state of inner poise born out of intuitive meditation.

And meditation does not mean a sitting down "meditation" in particular. You could be "meditating" while doing any activity or work. Just as Arjun is asked to be a yogi even on the battlefield, so too can we be yogis in whatever we are doing. That is the ultimate meaning of yoga. Else, yoga is pointless! Yoga is simply technique if we look at it in a narrow perspective. But looking at it in the perspective that Krishna is talking about is to understand that true Yoga is about taking flight to the higher skies and upper limits of self. There, you feel free. There, you move towards the state of Moksha or freedom, liberation of mind-body-spirit. It is both profound and practical. It is both a lesson for the material sphere as it is for the spiritual sphere.

Freeing yourself up spiritually automatically implies freeing up your mind, freeing up your heart. Therefore, at the level of thought and emotion also, you become free. And thereby, you become perfectly capable of taking on the tough times that life presents all living beings with at one stage or the other.

• 45 •

Bhakti Yoga: The Path of Devotion

CHAPTER TWENTY

Bhakti Yoga

Krishna says: "The person who is not changed by applause nor by blame, who is quiet and contented within, who has firm resolve of mind and is full of devotion, that person is indeed very dear to me!" Here, Krishna is summing up the very essence of Bhakti Yoga. Bhakti Yoga is a spontaneous attitude of devotion within all our functioning in life. It gives us an intuitive feel of oneness with the universe. And through that, we become immensely empowered with a spiritual power to take on all untoward situations in life, all crisis moments. We become filled with a great willpower and inner peace to be able to deal with tough times.

CHAPTER TWENTY-ONE

The Power of Devotion

Krishna enumerates the real qualities of the devotional person. Such a person is not affected by praise, nor by blame. Such a person has a silence within themselves. Such a person is content yet very firm in mind. That is the state of devotion! Krishna says: "The person who is free from dependence, who is crystal-clear, pure, untroubled, and non-anxious, and who has renounced the idea of results, such a person is the only one who can be truly devoted to me." Again, Krishna is emphasizing that we all need this attitude: whereby we are able to renounce our ego. So doing, we become independent, we become liberated. And at the same time, we become pure! That is the state which allows our innermost qualities to surface. And innermost qualities are what are needed during tough times; the highest of our inner qualities are needed. Devotion gives us great power during crises.

You have to disconnect from all that is happening on the surface of life and get connected with the innermost part of yourself. From there comes the current of universal force, universal energy. The real spirit of our being is within us. We are connected to the infinite through that spirit. There is no need to get overly anxious about what has happened on the outside. The world will go on as it is. Yes, there will be challenges. But at your essential core and crux, remember that you are joined to the highest truth as represented by the avatar Krishna.

All activity in life, all creativity in life, all great achievement in life is ultimately determined by the degree to which you can surrender yourself in a devoted attitude. Through the devoted attitude comes resilience. You can look at the example of great people across the ages. They all had a certain sense of devotion to whatever they did. They made their very work their worship. Even in the act of work, they devoted themselves. The idea is devotion itself. It's the devotional attitude! We may each have a different way of devotion. It is the inner attitude of surrendered devotion which makes you more powerful.

CHAPTER TWENTY-TWO

Surrender

Normally, in our worldly situations, we think "surrender" is something which the weak do. Surrendering is considered to be a sign of defeat. But in the realm of spirituality, "surrendering" is considered to be the most loving, the most empowering, the most deeply moving and energizing factor that you have in life. It allows you to move with cheer and hope; and most importantly, with optimism, even in the worst of times. With that inner attitude, you attain a degree of freedom, you attain a degree of inner greatness. And through inner greatness comes about joy in handling all sorts of situations; not only joy but calmness, tranquillity, the ability to be blissful, no matter what you are faced with.

On the battlefield of Kurukshetra, Krishna's disciple Arjun is faced with a great dilemma about whether to kill his enemies or whether to renounce the battle. Krishna explains to him that as long as there is devotion within Arjun's heart, he will be a force of good. So too must our attitude be! There are things we have to do in life. But remember, even in the midst of those things, you are to keep your sense of devotion intact. That is what joins you to Godhead, to the cosmic factor, to the greatest power that is making the galaxies rotate and the universe move ahead in its functioning.

CHAPTER TWENTY-THREE

Faith

Krishna says: "They are dear to me who consider me to be the supreme goal of life. Imbued with devotion and faith, they follow the real essence and nectar of religion." Krishna here is defining the very essence of the spiritual path. Real religion does indeed lie in faith, in devotion, but not blind faith! Krishna is implying a faith in a greater power, a sense of optimism, a sense of hope which catalyses the greatest within us.

Faith means that you are unshaken by whatever happens on the material sphere. You have the ability to transcend the suffering, the calamities, the idea of mental and physical harm on this material sphere. Those are inevitable: the human body has to eventually die. What is truly important is that you understand the idea that faith can transform your whole way of looking at things. Suddenly, through the power of faith, what seemed like a tough situation seems indeed not so tough anymore; because you know the power of the Greater is with you.

Mere intellectual and semantic logic does not suffice in filling man's spirit with wisdom, nor with fearlessness. And both wisdom and fearlessness are needed on the path to becoming a problem-solver during the toughest situations, because these qualities exist at the interior-most part of your being. Therefore, they give you the sense of being limitless.

CHAPTER TWENTY-FOUR

Strength

Usually, what happens during tough times is that we feel we don't have the strength to cope. That we don't have the power within us to deal with the situation. But suddenly, through the devotional attitude, you can find great clarity within your being. You find that quality which Krishna is talking about: "The person who is freed from both temporary happiness and anger, from fearfulness and anxiousness, such a person is dear to me." Again, Krishna is clarifying the quality of the person who is of the devotional attitude. A truly devotional person is not carried away through the material happiness of the world, nor is such a person disturbed by anger. Anger comes and goes in us all: sometimes, it is a useful tool to get things done. But don't let the anger within you, don't let the fear and anxiousness shake you to such an extent that you are unable to deal with circumstances in a cool and calm manner.

Devotion is the path which allows you to be strengthened through inner feelings of coolness and calmness, of going through the fire of challenges and coming out victorious. Krishna explains it his way. He says: "Just as gold is purified in fire, so too does the mind through devotion become pure in its material work and attains the highest reality. The mind of a person who is constantly thinking only of material objects, becomes attached to them. But the mind of the person who is devoted to me and merges with me, finds unity." Krishna is again talking about how we all have to go through the "fire" of material life. Yet, the mind which can go through that fire, and yet retain its devotion, is the mind which attains unity. And ultimately, unity—a oneness of feeling that we are joined to the greater reality of the cosmos and to the ultimate power—is the whole aim of all yoga.

CHAPTER TWENTY-FIVE

The Power of the Subtle

Krishna's implication is that he is beyond the most subtle also. So you can well imagine the infinite power of that. And here's the most interesting thing: science is coming more and more to the understanding that the more subtle a thing, the more powerful it is. Unfortunately, that often takes on a pernicious form: for example, the pandemics created by viruses. Viruses are very small entities, yet what destructive power they have! They can bring the whole of human civilization to its knees. They can create such difficult circumstances for us. But what Krishna is saying that he is the subtle-most: far beyond the range and power of any material entity. So our only refuge is to go to him; because the more subtle the element you seek, the more power you become imbued with.

The only solutions to the toughest problems in life are subtle solutions. Outer solutions alone will not work. They may work for the moment, but the ultimate entity, the final refuge, has to be the subtle-most entity. And Krishna represents the subtle-most entity. The story of his sheltering the people of Braj under the Govardhan Hill when Indra's wrath was inflicted through thunderstorms, is really metaphorical: it tells us that Krishna is our ultimate "shelter". The Lord is indeed our ultimate shelter. The universal energy behind the universe is our greatest shelter. We must all come under his refuge! Then any "storm" in life, any dark night in life is not enough to break us: because we are under the protection of that subtle power—that infinite being who makes all things come forth. In that situation, our mental effort is not needed. That is proved by what happens during crisis situations.

Gyaan Yoga: The Path of Knowledge

CHAPTER TWENTY-SIX

Gyaan Yoga

Krishna is creating clarity within Arjun through his teachings in the Bhagavad Gita. Later, as recounted in the Mahabharat, Krishna again teaches Arjun through the Anu Gita and the Uttara Gita. The essence of the teachings is on the "Yoga of Knowledge": Gyaana Yoga (also often spelled Jnana Yoga). The key to Gyaana Yoga is clarity. Such crystal-clarity of perception and of being that the doubts within one melt, and one's consciousness flows swift and free! This is very important in order to face life's untoward circumstances with great energy, wisdom, and non-impulsive power.

With clarity comes real energy. With clarity comes brilliance. With clarity comes courage. With clarity come all those virtues which take us towards successful living. Without clarity, we are simply in a state of confusion, as Arjun is before Krishna's teachings to him. And Arjun's problem is the problem with our modern civilization! While we have achieved such heights of affluence and material progress, modern man is completely unclear when it comes to the spiritual domain. His mind is troubled just as Arjun's mind is troubled. We are confused. Life should not be only about survival, but about living our lives more fruitfully and successfully in mind-body-spirit. That needs to be the new paradigm for human beings. Else, we keep hurtling from one crisis to another without addressing the roots of the problem: thereby triggering more anxiety. The way of silently imbibing the truth-consciousness-bliss of the divine aspect of life, is Krishna's way of Gyaana Yoga. It equips us to adequately move past tough times.

Sage-like clarity is the hallmark of Gyaana Yoga. Strengthening our determination to experience life with luminosity, clearness, and grace, is Gyaana Yoga in essence.

We can keep having more and more things in life, but without the beauty and energy of clarity in our mind, we don't feel that life is lived successfully. And in fact, that is entirely true in Arjun's case: he has become miserable because of this un-clarity. His energy has become dissipated. His energy has made him feel negative instead of feeling positive about life. And that's because his energy has moved towards a non-meditative state, a state where it is agitated. Krishna is bringing Arjun's energy to a state of meditativeness, of devotion, of dynamism. So this is the key thing to understand. Clarity comes about when your energy moves towards a meditative state, when your energy moves to a state where it is integrated, coming from deep within you, without agitation . . . when it comes out of a quiet mind, a quiet heart, a quiet being within yourself. That is the kind of energy which creates truly successful living.

So, that should be our aspiration, not about winning success at any cost. No! That will just be transitory. True success happens when your whole being is in integration, when both mind and heart are experiencing a sense of peace, a sense of blissful togetherness. And when in your innermost being, you feel an integration of all your higher virtues, all your higher energies working in tandem together. That creates the sort of peaceful clarity and understanding that is required for dynamism in life. And that is the kind of dynamism which Krishna is trying to infuse into Arjun. This helps Arjun vastly in coming out of the tough situation he is in mentally.

Krishna is not telling Arjun to go and fight the battle in a feverish state of being, an impassioned or angry state of being. He could have provoked Arjun into getting angry. He could have said: see, these enemies of yours on the battlefield have created so much chaos for you and your family, so fight them! But Krishna never tells him all that.

CHAPTER TWENTY-SEVEN

Trapped in Thoughts

Arjun has fallen into an abyss of thought, and the thought has itself become a trap. He's woven a spider's web of thoughts, and he's gotten trapped in that spider's web. And that is what we all keep doing, especially during perplexing situations such as crisis moments. We keep spinning our thoughts like the spider's web and we keep getting trapped in that same web of thoughts. There is no way out of it. It is only the quiet mind, it is only the calm mind, it is only the tranquil mind which does not weave that web of thoughts and hence, is never caught in the trap of thought or mind. It is able to perceive a higher reality. And so doing, it finds itself in a luminous, clear state of being. It finds itself in a state of being which is not ruled by the ego, but which can rather find direction from the universal flow of reality, which can take its cues from the larger aspects of reality.

Man is a very small part of this largeness of reality. We should not confuse ourselves to be the bodily complex, nor the egoic complex. And it is only people who can understand the sense of greater wisdom through something which is beyond them, through something which is greater than them, who become true visionaries and mavericks in life because they're able to see a higher vista, a greater truth. So we can see that the power of clarity means opening new dimensions of life, being able to look at life with a new dimension of vision. That takes us beyond whatever we have known: beyond our conditioned knowledge/thoughts/impressions/perceptions. And going beyond previous conditioned impressions and thought perceptions is the only way we can do something new in life. It is the only way we can go behind the curtain of Maya, as it were—Maya being the illusionary force of existence, as Krishna says in the Bhagavad Gita—and find that we are part of a far greater reality which is of the nature of Sat-Chit-Ananda, or truth-consciousness-bliss.

This trinity of themes, truth-consciousness-bliss, is in a way the entirety of the Bhagavad Gita. Krishna is, in effect, saying that within Arjun is all truth, all consciousness, and all bliss. Arjun's only problem is that he has forgotten it. And forgetting it, he has become dis-identified with these virtues of truth, consciousness, and bliss. And has instead, become identified with the web of thought. And that spider web of thought has taken him more and more away from truthful living, from consciousness-based living, from blissful living. Hence, the whole quality of his life is suffering. Hence, he is not able to find the true success of his life. Krishna is opening up Arjun's heart and mind to new sources of truth.

Krishna is, in effect, telling Arjun to come out of all that he has known, to come out of the darkness of his mind, to see the light of the divine. That light of the divine is playing through every atom of the universe, but we're not able to have the vision to look at it because we usually see everything through the lens of ego, through the lens of thought. And that lens is dusty. That lens is unclear. It's not allowing us to look with clarity. Instead, it's making us fearful, it's raising anxiety in the mind.

The only way to move towards greater vision and greater success in life is to feel a fullness of clarity, and the fullness of energy, together. And both things are missing in Arjun upon the battlefield. If he is able to bring more clarity, and thereby generate more energy within himself, the problem is solved. And that is what actually happens by the end of the Bhagavad Gita.

Not only does Krishna make him more clear in consciousness, but Arjun feels filled with a strange energy within. He feels fresh. It's like the words of the Gita wash him clean of the dust of thoughts. He feels like he's come back to his self-nature. He feels like once again he is that original being which he is meant to be. And that is the beauty of the Gita. It takes us away from this artificial being that we have created around ourselves, that artificial sense of personality which is a product of thought. We think we are a name, we are a person, a personality, and so on, which others refer us to. But actually, we are not that. We are of a greater self-nature. We are of a great inner freedom.

CHAPTER TWENTY-EIGHT

Decisiveness

Don't let the unclarity of your past conditioning, your past thoughts, hinder your primal clarity and energy. If you're not hindered by that, you come to meaningfulness in life, you come to purposefulness in life. And that is the only way to be decisive. This is another problem: Arjun has become indecisive! You see, it's like Hamlet in the play by William Shakespeare. Hamlet is an indecisive character. He keeps wondering, "To be or not to be, that is the question!" He is not able to commit himself to anything. He's not able to decide one way or the other. And that takes him towards doom. Arjun is doing the same thing: he's moving towards doom because of his indecisiveness. And this indecisiveness has happened because he's caught in the spider web of thought. To be indecisive during crisis moments and tough times is the most debilitating thing.

Krishna is giving Arjun an altogether different perspective. Krishna is teaching Arjun that his thoughts have no real ultimate meaning; because there is a greater light of soul within us, there is a greater light of unconditioned ideation of greater reality. That is pure consciousness. That is pure truth. That is pure bliss. Reflect that light of consciousness and truth and bliss. And then only does your life become truly successful. As long as we are not able to perceive the light of the greater, all our activities are in vain. What utility is there in any of our activities? They keep making us miserable, they keep making us joyless. The real joy of life is when you function effortlessly. But you are never able to function effortlessly if you look at everything through the prism of your egoistic thoughts. That only creates unclarity, that only creates lack of energy. And then, whatever you do, does not come out of your heart. It does not come out of the quietness of your mind. It does not have the quality of devotion.

In other words, you feel depleted in energy. And then whatever you do is not genuine, because it's not coming out of the genuine part of your being. Krishna is reminding Arjun that within him is the element of the macrocosm, within him is the element of the ultimate! He is telling Arjun to listen to that element alone, to go with that will of the greater. And when he goes with the will of the greater, he is able to find his true mission in life; he finds his freedom. You see, we think we are independent in thought. But the problem is our thoughts are similar to what society thinks, to what others think. Thoughts are a product of social conditioning, thoughts are a product of educational conditioning, and often of religious conditioning too.

CHAPTER TWENTY-NINE

The Cosmic Mind

Krishna is taking Arjun away from all this conditioning. And only people who are able to get away from this conditioned thought are able to be true innovators, true creators in life. That is the natural way. The unnatural way is to identify with conditioned thoughts and make the mistake of thinking that is our reality. That never allows the inner being of ourselves to flower, that never allows the ultimate energy of ourselves to come to the substance, to come to fruition. We keep running around in circles. We keep thinking that we should function according to the dictates of our own mind. But Krishna is telling Arjun that behind the individual mind lies this immensity of the cosmic mind, the divine mind. And that mind is the ultimate doer. Ultimately, our own minds are only an instrument of that greater cosmic mind. Our mind is only a partial reflection of that greatness which brings about the galaxies, the stars, the nebulae and so on.

We are a simple drop in that cosmic sea. Knowing ourselves to be a drop in that cosmic sea, we can dissolve into it and feel one with it. And then, the whole energy of the cosmic sea becomes ours. Then there's no need to feel hopeless, there's no need to feel afraid, there's no need to feel anxious; because for the first time you come to understand that the power of the entire, the power of the ultimate is within you. And when you feel that, not only do you attain great energy, a great flowing energy and clarity within yourself, but a very great confidence within yourselves.

Most people feel a lack of confidence during tough times, naturally. So-called confidence in life, so-called positive thinking often does not help when it comes to the crunch. Only the confidence of the silent mind, the quiet heart—full of the light of consciousness, truth, and bliss—is the powerful confidence! That takes you closer to your self-nature. That brings you into an intimate connection with your greater powers. And through that, you're not only able to relax into your self-nature. You are also able to cut out all the roots of anxiety which exist within you. All those apprehensions about what you can do and can't do in life, about what will happen tomorrow, all that dissolves. Then you realize that you can do everything in a state of bliss. You can do everything in a state of freedom, everything in a state of great power: because you are functioning naturally. You are not enslaved by the trap of your own thoughts. You come into a situation where all the tasks that you do have become devotional, become prayerful, just like Arjun's very act of battle moves towards the devotional act. He starts identifying with the cosmic mind that Krishna represents. That pulls him out of the morass of the tough situation.

The ultimate warrior is one who can fight in a state of identification with the higher cosmic mind, and not be hemmed in by small individuality and its concomitant apprehensions. In a state of reverence to the cosmic mind, the power of the greater comes to the warrior. The true warrior never feels alone! He feels that the cosmic factor is ever with him!

The core idea of Gyaana Yoga is this: identifying with the greater cosmic consciousness. When you do that, you find real courage. And with real courage comes real clarity. It is all about an idea of dropping the fear from yourself. But fear can never be dropped as long as you identify with your smaller self. You have to identify with the larger cosmic energy which exists within you. Then you find yourself more energetic. You find yourself more potential-realized, because the circle of self undergoes a change. You no longer identify with the old person that you thought you were. Suddenly you find that you are part of a greater reality.

CHAPTER THIRTY

No Limits, No Boundaries

Krishna is essentially telling Arjun that there are no boundaries that we need to put on ourselves. Arjun has put this great boundary upon himself—that he is part of a particular clan, that he should not harm the members of his clan.

Krishna is saying: there are no boundaries. The only boundaries which exist are within our minds. If you can move forward from those boundaries of mind, you become free: you suddenly belong to the greater dimension! You are not then identifying with any particular race or caste or colour or clan. Look at yourself as being beyond all that. Then only do you come to your greater reality. Then only does your action become more dynamic. And then only do you find a complete realization of your innate potential. Through such knowledge, Arjun suddenly realizes that yes, he's indeed greater than he thought he was. He's indeed far more than the human being he thought he was. He, in fact, does not belong to any particular race, region, or clan. He is able to go past all geopolitical thinking, all boundaried and walled-up thinking. He's able to look at himself as being of the purity of soul. And so doing, he becomes fearless, clear, dynamic. And so doing, he is able to achieve the greatest success of life.

All these things become important when it comes to successful living. It is simply a question of enjoying yourself at the highest degree, through dropping this idea that you have limitations upon yourself. In your most natural state, you have no limitations. In your most natural state, you are as much a part of the divine as any other being. You carry all the potential of the divine within you. Seeing that itself takes you into a dynamism and makes you flow towards more successful action in life. What holds you back is this anxiety that you are limited. It is this anguish: that you have to live within certain limitations. Krishna is telling Arjun that in his innermost core, there exists the divine. In fact, there he—Krishna—himself exists! So, identify with that core within which the divine exists. If you can do that, you move towards soulful living.

CHAPTER THIRTY-ONE

Being Neutral

Krishna is telling Arjun to relax into the greater consciousness, to relax into the greater soulfulness of life, and forget about the anxiety of thought, because thought never allows you to be relaxed. It has too much baggage within it. It carries all the baggage and fears of the yesterday which provoke a fear within the present moment. Much of our thought is dominated by the darkness of what has gone behind us as our past.

Yes, if you can think perfectly clearly, there's no problem. If you can think without any background knowledge and memory obscuring your perception, that is good. That is called objective thinking. That is very good thinking. That is the hallmark of the greatest thinkers. But most of us, when we dwell upon a subject, would find that there's too much past baggage also coming in the way, too many feelings associated with certain subjects, with certain relationships, with certain aspects of our life and work. Hence, Krishna is saying: you can get away from all that. Simply identify with the higher principle, and then you're free of the past. You move towards a greater freedom. You move towards a non-tension, a non-contraction of your energy. And when you are able to move towards a non-tension of energy, your natural energy surfaces more strongly. You are then able to act spontaneously and energetically. You are able to act with clarity, and with a higher degree of devotion/passion in whatever you do.

So doing, your results are bound to be of a higher and greater nature. You are able to manifest more value into the world because you're functioning as an integrated individual whose thoughts, actions, and aspirations are all in tandem. A person who can do that creates an integration between impulses and their realization, and is thereby able to create a greater beauty of energy within life. Not only does that person do their work with more genuineness, with more power and more passion, but people find charisma and an inward integrity coming through. And such people are bound to become great leaders in life, which is what Krishna again reminds Arjun of. He urges Arjun because people look at Arjun as a leader, he is to act like one! A leader is supposed to act with absolute crystal-clarity and absolute calmness, particularly in tough situations. That is one of the hallmarks of great leadership. That leads to a confidence in decision-making ability. A clear leader is a decisive leader. In the same way, a clear leader is an energetic leader.

Ultimate Warrior Consciousness

The Bhagavad Gita teaches the warrior's way of spiritually fearless living. Through it, Krishna addresses the needs of body, mind, and soul. Each of us is to imbibe the ultimate warrior-consciousness outlined in the Gita. The rule is this: if you give of yourself through the best of your consciousness, there is nothing more to be concerned about. Then everything you receive or achieve in life is a blessing. Through this attitude of warriorhood, you become capable of taking on all challenges in life.

So it all begins and ends with our state of consciousness. Focus on that. The life, legends, and teachings of Krishna stand as the biggest testament to living life in an exalted state of warrior-consciousness.

Krishna's "way of the warrior" is applicable to all aspects of life and living. It contains mystic keys to a healthy consciousness, and is therefore for all walks of life. Through understanding Krishna, you can face any crisis or untoward circumstance with confidence. You can face even death with joy. That is the right way to deal with tough times: keeping a spirit full of optimism and good cheer.

Fear, anxiety, and apprehension can be mankind's most debilitating weaknesses. They can make us feel limited in potential, and give rise to all sorts of complexes. They engender all sorts of crisis situations within our consciousness and also in "real life". Jealousy, hatred, narrow-mindedness, and so on are some of their by-products. Freedom from fear/worry/anxiety is one of the most essential longings of mankind. It is the timeless need of human beings everywhere, universally important. Krishna's treasures of insight root out negative aspects of consciousness, making it powerful and pristine. They dynamize bliss within the soul.